JN439849

Theresa Hyun

시인 현태리

판문점에서의 차 한잔

A Cup of Tea at P’anmunjom

현태리 시집

Theresa Hyun Book of Poetry

판문점에서의 차 한잔

A Cup of Tea at P'anmunjom

Poetics 시학

■ 시인의 말

시는 나에게 특별한 의미가 있다. 왜냐하면 시 낭송은 어릴 적에 어머니께서 항시 들려주던 낭랑한 소리였기 때문이다. 어머니는 유년 시절에 나에게 시의 의미를 새겨 주셨다. 나는 프랑스 니스 대학교에서 시를 공부했다. 그리고 서울에서 살면서 한국 젊은이들이 시집을 즐겨 읽는 것을 보았다. 한국인들이 자국의 문학을 사랑하고 그 전통을 아끼는 것을 알았다. 이 속에서 생활하면서 한국인들의 시를 사랑하는 정서를 배우고 삶의 방식에 빠져들었다. 이러한 한국인들의 시를 사랑하는 정서에 나는 동참했다.

1990년에 들어서면서 시와시학사 사람들과 어울렸다. 그들에게 많은 영감을 받았다. 특히 원로 시인들에게 시에 대해 많은 것을 배웠다. 여기에 발표한 시들은 지난 20년간 이들과 어울려 지내면서 창작한 시편들이다. 여기에 수록된 시들은 특별히 한국에 살면서 한국인들의 삶의 고통과 변화하는 생활의 모습에 같이 동참하면서 그것을 반영한 시편들이다. 요즘의 정서 속에서 살아가는 젊은 독자들은 과거의 한국 생활의 정서에 다소 생소함을 느낄 수도 있을 것이다. 그러나 이것은 빠르게 사라져 가는 우리들의 정서를 시편에 담은 것으로 그 의미를 찾아야 할 것이다. 그러므로 이 시집은 세월이 흐르면서 그 의미를 더해 갈 수 있다고 생각한다.

이 시집에 실린 모든 시편들은 원래 한국어로 창작하였다. 그리고 모든 시어들은 한국 고유의 언어 묘사로 써진 것이다. 그러나 한국 시를 배우고 좋아하는 외국인들이 한국 정서가 담긴 시에 쉽게 접할 수 있도록 한국어 시편들을 영어로 동시 번역했다. 또한 한국 정서를 영어로 묘사하려는 한국 시인들을 위해서 한국어 시편들을 영어로 번역했다. 그러므로 시적 언어 표현의 미숙함과 한계성을 보일 수도 있을 것이다. 이러한 일련의 노력이 쌓여서 후에 더 나은 한국 시와 번역시가 나오기를 바라는 마음으로 두 언어로 시집을 출간하였다. 나의 첫 시집인 이 책의 출간을 통해 앞으로 심오하고 더 좋은 시편들을 수록한 미래의 시집들이 출간되기를 희망한다.

『시와시학』의 신인 당선에 추천해 주신 고은 선생님의 은혜에 깊은 감사를 드립니다. 아울러 수년 동안 지도해 주시고 격려를 아끼지 않으신 김재홍 선생님께도 깊은 감사의 말씀을 드립니다. 나의 첫 시집의 삽화를 손수 그려 주신 천부적인 재능을 소유한 전하리 선생에게도 깊은 감사를 드립니다. 이 시집은 계간『시와시학』의 여러 편집인들의 도움과 헌신이 없었더라면 출간될 수 없었을 것이기에 이 모든 분들께도 감사의 말씀을 전합니다. 또한 그동안 시 창작을 하는 나의 모습을 줄곧 지켜보면서 격려를 아끼지 않으신 가족들과 친구들과 캐나다한인문인협회 회원들께도 깊은 감사의 말씀을 전합니다.

■ Foreward

Poetry has always been an important part of my life, from my early childhood days when I heard my mother read her favorite works, to my experiences as an exchange student in Nice studying French authors. When I arrived in Seoul I was impressed with the eagerness of young people to obtain the latest volumes by well-known poets, and I realized that Koreans have a deep respect and admiration for their literary traditions. As I struggled to overcome the complexities of a new life, I became aware that poetry offers a key to understanding Korean language and culture.

Since the early 1990s I have been taking part in the classes and activities of Si wa Sihak (Poetry and Poetics) where I have received support and inspiration from mentors and fellow students. I have written the poems in this volume over a period of almost twenty years, and they reflect both my evolving impressions and the changes in Korean life. The reader may find that some of the works depict scenes which have become rare in contemporary Korea and share my sense of nostalgia about aspects of our society which are fast vanishing.

Originally I wrote all the poems in Korean, and I have translated some of them into English for the benefit of Korean readers who might want to hear another aspect of my voice, as well as for those who are interested in Korean poetry but are unable to read the language. I am well aware of the limits of my language skills, and I hope that my first volume of poetry will be followed by others which will be more meaningful and of higher quality.

I am deeply grateful to poet Ko Un for his graciousness in recommending me for the Si wa Sihak New Poet Award, and to Professor Kim Jay-Hong for his guidance and encouragement over the years. I feel very fortunate that Chon Ha-Ri has been willing to employ her exceptional talents in illustrating this volume. This work would not have been possible without the dedication of the Si wa Sihak staff. I would also like to acknowledge the help provided by family, close friends and the members of the Korean Canadian Writers' Association.

목 차 Table of Contents

판문점에서의 차 한잔

금강산은 부른다

먹구름 덮인 산속으로
하늘 갈매기 한 떼 날아가네요
아, 새들만 갈 수 있나요
구름만 갈 수 있나요

쇌쇌 쇌쇌
들쑥날쑥한 바닷가 모래를 따라서
밀물에 휩쓸려
썰물에 떠내려
바위로 바위로 흐르며
파도로만 밀려가네요

그 이름 불러 불러도
아무 대답 없고
먼 산 넘어 빈 하늘에
구름만 떠가고 있네요

마을버스를 기다리며

한여름 햇볕 쨍쨍 은행나무 행렬 속에
공중전화 박스가 맴맴맴
금속성으로 울고 있네

세탁소 미용실 문방구점 여기저기
사람 사람마다 손바닥 귀에 대고
쉴 새 없이 저 혼자 웅얼웅얼 거리는데

느럭느럭 손수레 할멈만 다가와
쭈글쭈글 웃음사래치며 전화하시네

오늘은 반가운 손님이 오시겠네

Waiting for the Village Bus

Midsummer sunbeams scorching, glaring
In the line of Ginkgo trees
The public telephone booth
Chirps a metallic cry.

Launderette, Beauty Shop, Stationery Store, back and forth
Each and everyone cups a hand to the ear
All muttering to themselves.

Only the handcart Grandma draws near the booth
Slowly, slowly with a crinkled smile.

Today a welcome guest comes.

1. 2. 3 약국

온갖 아픔 진전시키는
우리 동네 안창식 약사

감기 기침 배탈 신경통
어린 투정 오랜 고민
하루도 빠짐없이
사알살 달래는 약손

이 시대의 울화병
누그러뜨리는 1. 2. 3 약국

1. 2. 3 Pharmacy

Soothing all sorts of aches

Our neighbourhood pharmacist, An Ch' ang-Sik

Colds, coughs, indigestion, nervous tension

Childish grumbling, lingering distress

Everyday without exception

Gently stroking medicine hands

Calm the pent-up feelings of our time

1. 2. 3 Pharmacy

마음의 꽃다발

먼 곳으로 떠나셨나
말도 흔적도 없이

북망산천 가는 길이
서럽고도 서러울 텐데
굳센 마음으로 가셨네

아버님의 집이 텅 비어 있다
그러나 앞마당에 향내 풍기는 백합들
하나하나 거두어들이고
올려드립니다

그새 하얀 열매들
늘 품고 있는
작은 꽃다발

A Bouquet of the Heart

He left for a far-away place
Without a word or a trace.

Although the path to Pukmang Sanch' on*
Would be sorrowful and grievous
He went with a steadfast spirit.

Father' s house is bare.
Yet one by one
I gather the fragrant lilies in the front yard
And offer them up.

Those pure white blossoms
I always keep in my heart,
A small bouquet of flowers.

---

* Traditionally in Korea this was thought to be the place where people went after death.

애착

무슨
날개 펴기 위해서인가
이른 아침
미풍에 떨리는 자작나무 잎을
애벌레 한 마리
그렇게 붙잡고 있네
바람에
떨고 있네

Devotion

Grasping like that
The white birch leaf
Quivering in the morning breeze

For the sake of
Spreading what wings
Is the caterpillar
Trembling in the wind?

갈대

홀로
산기슭을 걷는다
날카로운 가을바람에
갈밭을 지나고
낙엽을 밟는다
잊어버리자고

하늘거리는 갈대도
홀로
흔들리고 있다

잊을 수 있을까? 나는

샘터

샘솟듯
셀 수 없는
주산, 서예, 웅변, 외국어, 피아노
속셈 학원
하루 종일 쉬지도 않고
어린아이 울리는 터
샘 많은 세상에
동네 아이들도
쫓아가는
셈

지게꾼

초여름 햇볕에
포일 마을* 온통 부글거리고 있네
지붕 사이사이로
가지런한 장독들 가물거리고

저 너머 논밭으로 땀에 젖은 지게꾼
느릿느릿 긴 역사를 짊어지고 가네

* 포일 마을 : 경기도 안양시의 마을 이름.

An A-Frame* Carrier

In the early summer sunlight
All of P' oil village simmers
Among the rooftops
Neat rows of soy sauce jars glimmer

Over there across the paddy fields, drenched in sweat
An A-Frame carrier
Step by step shoulders his long history.

* A wooden device which is strapped on the back and used for carrying packages.

고구마 할미

겨울 내내
네거리에

찬바람 퇴근길에 고구마 좀 사려 하니
할머니 웃으면서 천 원어치 골라 주네

겨울 내내
네거리에

머얼리 눈 덮인 산 바라보면
옛사람 옛이야기 생각나네

겨울 내내
네거리에

거스름 돈 쥐어 주는 군고구마 같은 손
그냥 웃으며 하염없이 살아가네

Sweet Potato Grandma

All winter long
At the crossroads

Coming home from work in the biting wind, I stop to buy some sweet potatoes.
Smiling, Grandmother picks out 1000 won worth.

All winter long
At the crossroads

As she gazes at the far-away snow covered mountain
People of bygone days, old stories come to mind.

All winter long
At the crossroads

Hands like roasted sweet potatoes give out change.
Still smiling she idles her time away.

스님의 가르침

항상

깨어날 때----자명종, 아침 뉴스

항용

집 나갈 때----뚝딱뚝딱 이웃집 아침 식사 준비
　　　　　　　으르렁 출근 차들

가끔

등산할 때----머얼리 매미, 뻐꾹 울음소리

어쩌다

계곡을 향할 때----가까이 샘물 바람 소리

그 순간----들리네 참으로 들리네
　　　　　　내 영혼의 소리

A Buddhist Priest' s Teaching

Usually

When I wake up - - - the alarm clock, morning news

Ordinarily

When I leave the house - - - ticking, pattering, the neighbour' s breakfast preparation

the rumble of cars leaving for work

Occasionally

When I climb mountains - - - from afar the chirping of cicadas, cuckoos

By chance

When I head towards a valley - - - nearby the sound of spring water, of wind

In that moment - - - I can hear it, I can really hear it

the sound of my spirit.

만추晩秋

어둑어둑 해 저물고
울적한 거리를 걸으면
집집마다 어슴푸레 불을 밝히네

날카로운 늦가을 바람에
낙엽들 우수수 떨어지고
아늑한 거실 가랑잎 사이로 엿보이네

지고 있는 그믐달 뒤로
웃음 울음 섞인 등불
머얼리 비추고 있네

오늘도 발길 멈추네
메마른 거리 모퉁이에서

Late Autumn

Dusky the day draws to a close.
As I walk along the gloomy road
Each and every house lights up a hazy lamp.

In the stinging late fall wind
The leaves rustle down.
And I steal a glance at a cozy sitting room
Through the dried up leaves.

Behind the waning moon
A lamp mixed with laughter and tears
Shines into the distance.

Today again I halt
At the withered street corner.

덕수궁 수수께끼

서울의 스핑크스인가

세종대왕 동상
오늘도 600년 세월
묵묵히 지켜 섰네

대한문
바깥세상
그토록 시끄러운데

빈 하늘 침묵만 지켜 섰네

The Riddle of Doksu Palace

Maybe it' s the sphinx of Seoul.

Still today the statue of King Sejong the Great*
Silently keeps watch over the passing of 600 years.

The world outside Taehan Gate
Is so clamorous.

He only watched over the silence of the empty sky.

---

* A fifteenth century early Choson dynasty King who was responsible for the creation of the Korean alphabet. His statue sits in the enclosed gardens of the ancient Doksu Palace, now in the center of downtown Seoul, capital of South Korea.

판문점에서의 차 한잔

1

관광객 꽉 찬 휴게소

오랜만에 형제끼리 모였다

진달래 활짝 핀 봄날 오후

2

인파의 소용돌이 속

큰형님 창밖을 내다본다

……저 북쪽 흐린 하늘

보이지 않는 얼굴

……아직도 살아 있을까

3

두런두런 이야기들 하는데

큰형님 훌쩍 마시네

눈물 한잔

A Cup of Tea at P' anmunjom*

At a resting place packed with tourists
The family gathered after a long time
On a spring afternoon azaleas in full bloom.

Amid the swirling crowd
Oldest brother gazes out the window.
--- That cloudy northern sky
Those missing faces
--- Could they still be alive?

As they whisper together
Oldest brother slowly sips
A tea cup full of tears.

---

* P' anmunjom Truce Village is located on the southern side of the demilitarized zone separating North and South Korea. It is a place where official negotiations are held between the two sides, and families from South Korea gather to remember the relatives they left behind in the North.

승무

1

이승에 태어날 때부터
저승길 가고 있군요

2

홍이 난 걸음으로
하늘을 접어 흔들고 있군요

3

어이! 저 양반
속도를 줄이시오

천안문天安門 연날리기

일요일이면
북경 사람들
연날리기하러 간다

하늘하늘
칼 같은 날개 훨훨 날아
시퍼런 창공에 솟아오른다
어디까지 올라갈 수 있을까

언제까지 참을 수 있을까
높이높이
쇠갈퀴 손들 연줄을 당기며
핏빛 하늘 찔러 또 찔러
부끄러운 하늘 아래
대륙의 아우성 울려 퍼져

일요일이면
천안문 광장 차츰차츰 채워진다
저들 희망의 깃발로

Kite Flying at the Gate of Heavenly Peace

On Sundays
The people of Beijing
Go out to fly kites.

Lightly, buoyantly
Knife-like wings briskly fly.
They soar into the vivid blue heavens.
How high can they go?

How long can they endure?
Higher and higher
Iron hands pull the kite strings
Stabbing the reddening sky again and again.
Under the shameful sky
The cries of the land echo.

On Sundays
The Gate of Heavenly Peace Square fills up little by little
With the banners of their hopes.

서울 뒷골목

감나무 가지 사이로
안마당 빨랫줄
반짝반짝
아침 햇살 널려 있고

담장 너머
도붓장사 골목골목으로
근심 가득 실은 수레를 끌고 간다

A Back Alley in Seoul

Glistening, gleaming
Between the persimmon tree branches
Morning sun-rays spread over
The inner yard clothesline.

Beyond the wall, a peddler
Pulls along his handcart packed with troubles
From alley to alley

도선사에 돌다

바람이 분다
바람이 돈다
세차게 인수봉 넘어
이승과 저승이 이어진다

석불 옆 감나무 가지 흔들리고
처마 끝엔 풍경 소리 들려오고
목탁 휘파람새 솔바람새
울음소리 회오리바람
몸을 떨고

거세게 계곡으로 부는 바람
장사꾼들 허둥지둥
사람과 사람 사이를 스쳐 간다
그 마음 하늘 흔들린다

Circling Around Toson Temple

The wind blows.
The wind goes round
Powerfully crossing Insu Peak,
Linking this world and the next.

Beside the stone Buddha the persimmon tree branch sways.
I can hear the sounds of the wind bell at the tip of the eaves,
And the wooden gong, the willow warbler, the pine breeze bird,
Chirping, the whirlwind
Shaking my body.

The wind fiercely blowing through the valley
Brushes past the scurrying merchants,
Through the crowd
The sky spirit wavers.

독

뚜껑 덮인
천 달린 오지그릇에
둥글둥글 얼 밴 광택 나는
중배 부른 소박한 겉모습과
절인 배추 담는 내 모습을
발효시키는 효소들이
시詩의 참 독자이리

점쟁이를 찾아서

점쟁이를 찾아볼까요?

그래그래
돈암 고갯길 아래
매연 속 얼핏 보이는
팔자 신수 궁합 간판의 숲
들여다볼까요?

언제나 문은 열려 있고
안방에 그윽이
사주책 잡은 손 더듬더듬
오십 평생 눈먼 세월
손으로 한번 볼까요?

앞길 어두컴컴하니
걸음걸이 밝히자
때로는 만 오천
때로는 이만 원어치 사주팔자를 산다

생生의 바다 등불을 찾아볼까요?

Visiting a Fortune-teller

Shall we visit a fortune-teller?

Yes, all right
At the bottom of Donam pass*
Glimpsed through the smog
A forest of billboards — destiny, fortune, marital harmony
Shall we stop by?

The door is always open.
In the inner quarters, quietly
The hands holding the fortune-telling book touch and finger
A fifty-year lifetime passed in blindness
Shall we see by hand?

The path ahead is somber
So let' s brighten our step.

At times we buy 15,000
At times 20,000 won worth of fortune.

Shall we visit the lamplight of life' s ocean?

---

* Donam pass is near an area of the city of Seoul which is noted for fortune-tellers, some of whom are blind.

성묘하는 날

터벅터벅 줄지어 가네
산길 높이높이
근심 걱정 보따리
하나씩들 지고 가네

맴맴 솔바람에
매미 울음 흔들려 흔들려
뽑고 뜯고 베어져서
몸져누운 잡초들
시드는 향기 그윽이 맑아서
소나기 온 뒤
새 세상 같네

무덤 앞에 고요히 머리 숙이니
향 내음 풍겨 와 떠오르는
어머니의 흰 적삼
못 다한 말 속삭임으로 들려오네
우리 삶의 얼룩진 고달픔

씻어 버리네

갓난아기 새 세상 같네

A Day at the Family Graves

Higher and higher
We trudge up the mountain path in a line,
Each carrying a bundle of worries and cares.

The chirring of the cicadas
Wavers in the pine breeze.
Plucking, weeding, hewing
The drooping weeds
The withered fragrance quietly refreshes
Like a clear world after a storm.

As we silently bow our heads in front of the graves
Mother' s white choksam*
Comes to mind with the fragrance of incense.
Whisperings of unfinished words can be heard.
The stained weariness of our life washes away.

Now the life of a new-born child.

---

* an unlined Korean summer jacket.

서울 테러리스트

험악한 삶의 길에
여러 가지 주의 사항

공사 중!
 과속 단속
  전용차선
   추월 금지
    속도를 줄이시오
     추락 주의!
      위험!

앞만 보고 달려도 앞 못 보는
자동인형들

한남대교
 반포대교
  성산대교
   행주대교

김포공항으로
세계를 향해

서울이 추락한다

Seoul Terrorists

On the rugged path of life
Various warnings

Under Construction!
 Speed Control Zone
  Restricted Vehicle Lane
   Passing Prohibited
    Reduced Speed
     Beware of Falling
      Danger!

Automatic dolls
Dash forward without seeing

Hannam Bridge
 Panp' o Bridge
  Songsan Bridge
   Haengju Bridge

Towards Kimp' o Airport

Heading for the world

Seoul is crashing.

동행

서초, 방배, 사당 역마다
조간신문을 옆구리에 낀
출근 행렬

바늘도 들어갈 틈 없는 열차 속
꽉 찼네 활짝 펼친 신문
펼쳐 든 신문 지면 속
내쳐지고 또 채워져

신촌, 이대, 시청 역마다
버려져 꾸깃꾸깃 내려져

파묻히는 일 속

Traveling Together

Socho, Pangpae, Sadang,* station after station
The queue on the way to work
Morning newspapers inserted under arms

The train is chockfull of spread out newspapers
Without an inch to breathe.
In the midst of the expanding pages
They are cast away and crammed in.

Shinch' on, Edae, Shich' ong, station after station
They' re thrown away, crumpled. They' re dropped off.

Buried in work.

---

* The Seoul subway inner circle line is one of the busiest, particularly during the morning and evening rush hours.

고향 길

차창 밖으로
따스한 별 하나
멀리 사라져 가고

이모는 자기 언니한테 간다고
팔십 평생 보듬어 주던
그 손길 찾아간다고

귀 대어 보면 아직도
우리 집 구석구석 들려오는
이모의 웃음소리

고운 별 하나 오늘도
어두운 밤하늘에
혼자 떠오르고 있네

The Way Home

Outside the train window
A warm star
Is vanishing far away.

Our Aunt said she was going to see her sister,
To seek the one who extended a helping hand
Through eighty years of life.

If you listen carefully, still
In every corner of the house
Our Aunt' s laughter can be heard.

Today a fine star
In the dark night
Rises alone.

바위

산마루 아파트 단지 한구석
옛 절 한 채
처마 끝에 솔바람 그윽이 이네

사찰 노송 아래 둥글 바위에
오랫동안 한숨 서려
방울방울 이슬로 스며들었네

고통의 눈물 노동의 땀방울
풀잎 타고 대대로 흘러내리고
오늘은 근심 보따리로 남아 있네

세상에서 가장 굳센 것은
풀잎처럼 여리고 약한 것인가
바위가 풀잎을 껴안는 그 마음인가

The Rock

Beside a mountainous apartment complex
An old temple
At the edge of the eaves there is a peaceful pine
breeze.

Steaming for a long time
Dew seeped drop by drop
Into the round rock behind the old temple pine.

Tears of suffering, sweat of toil
Are carried on a blade of grass and now and then
flow down
Today they remain as a bundle of cares.

The strongest thing in the world,
Is it something delicate like the blade of grass,
Or that spirit of the rock embracing every drop?

느티나무 비에 젖어

— 서울, 1998. IMF①

비에 젖고 있는 기중기
우두커니 서 있다 꾸부정히
저 아래 길거리를 내려다보는
느티나무, 낮고 구슬픈 빗소리에
귀 기울이고 있다
비에 젖은 사내처럼

A Rain-Drenched Zelkova Tree

A rain-drenched crane
Stands idly, slightly bent.
That Zelkova tree overlooking the street below
Listens carefully to the soft, sorrowful sound of the rain,
Like a rain-drenched man.

비

— 서울, 1998. IMF②

쏴쏴 장대비 쏟아져
고층 아파트에서 우듬지까지
천지만물이 울고 있는데
그 굵고 검은 몸통 앞에
담배만 애타게 태우는
한 젊은이
나뭇잎이 모진 눈물
한 방울 두 방울 받아들이고 있다

Rain

The swishing rain pours down.
From high-rise apartments to tree tops
Heaven, earth and all creation weep.
In front of that thick, dark trunk
A young man anxiously smoking cigarettes
Receives the merciless tears one by one.

장마
— 서울, 1998. IMF③

뿌리도 정처도 없는
한 떠돌이
땅속으로 깊이 내린
수백 년 달콤 씁쓸한 노래
마음으로 듣고 있다
빗속에 서성거리고 있다

Rainy Season

Without roots or destination
A wanderer
Listens wholeheartedly to the bitter-sweet ancient song
Rooted deep in the earth.
Restlessly she paces back and forth in the rain.

9월의 썰물

콕콕콕
지칠 줄 모르는 호미 소리
초가을 오후를 울린다
여기저기 개펄을 찌르고 찔러

여름내 살 오른 아이들
        따스한 햇볕
            철썩거리는 물결 따라
                모두 다 휩쓸려가고

하루 종일 거둔 가득한 조개 가마니
제부도* 아낙네들
살살살
저녁노을로 흐르는 삶

---

* 제부도 : 경기도 화성면 서해안에 있는 섬.

September Ebb Tide

Piercing, thrusting, poking,
The tireless sound of the weeding hoe
Echoes in the early fall afternoon
Here and there stabbing the slime.

The youngsters, thriving all through the summer
The mild warmth of the sunbeams
Everything is swept away
With the splashing surf.

A straw bag packed with clams, gathered throughout the day
The women-folk of Chebu Island
Slowly slowly
Their lives flow towards the sunset.

토론토 12월의 거리에서

첫눈 오는 밤거리
발자국 따라가는데
문득 사라져 버리네
뒷골목조차 없는 이 도시
하얗게 덮여 있어

이 밤거리
내 언 손 감싸 주던
너의 입김
틈조차 없는 이 세상 밖으로
희미해져 가고 있네

눈길에 남아 있어
너의 새하얀 그림자

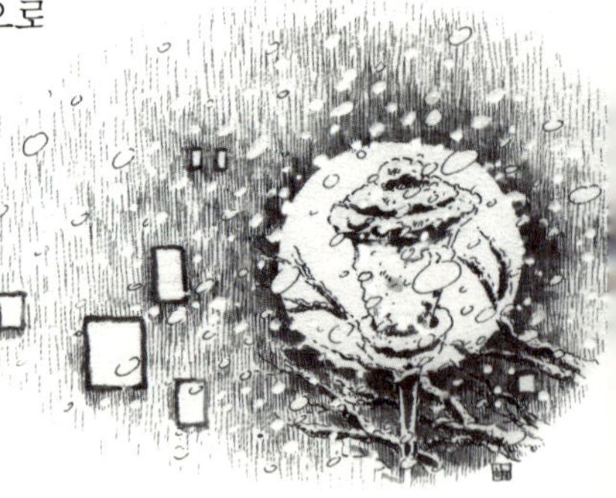

On a Toronto Street in December

On a night street as the first snow falls
I follow the footprints.
Unexpectedly they fade away.
This city without even a back alley
Is covered in white.

On this night street
Enveloping my frozen hands
Your breath
Becomes misty
In this world without even a gap.

Your pure white shadow
Remains on the snow-covered street.

그 여자와 그 남자

아, 벌써 6시네

커피 컵 치우고
재떨이 닦고
전등 낮추고
립스틱 바르고
머리 만지고
재빨리 하루를 갈아입는
그 여자

챙긴 일보다
쟁여 있는 일 더 많은데
마음 달래기 어려운 괴로움
술 술 술로
퇴근길 단골집 들르는
그 사내

술잔 주고받는 거품 같은

입맞춤
실컷 마셔 버리는
고단한 하루
또 하루

That Man and That Woman

Oh, it' s already 6 o' clock.

Clearing away the coffee cups
Wiping the ashtrays
Dimming the lights
Putting on lipstick
Fixing her hair
Nimbly changing the day' s outfit
That woman

The inbox is piled higher than the outbox.
Troubles he can' t get off his mind
Booze booze booze
Stopping by his favorite bar on the way home
That fellow

Exchanging beer glasses
A frothy kiss

Guzzling down to their hearts' s content

One weary day after another

색소폰 솔로

해 질 녘
1305호 발코니를 울리는
달콤 씁쓸한 노래
점점 희미해져 가고
별들만 듣고 있네

때론 속삭임보다 더 부드럽게
때론 아우성보다 더 날카롭게
달빛맞이 가락으로
껴안고 울고 있네

으스름달밤
산마루 아파트 단지 한구석에
일그러진 사나이
세레나데 바쳐도
아무 대답 없네

달빛만 눈 뜨고 듣고 있네
별들만 귀 열고 듣고 있네

Saxophone Solo

Toward nightfall
The bittersweet song
Sounding on no. 1305 balcony
Grows faint little by little.
Only the stars listen.

At times more softly than a whisper
At times more piercing than an outcry
In tune with the moonlight
They embrace singing.

A hazy moonlight night
In a corner of a mountainous apartment complex
A twisted fellow
Although he offers a serenade
There is no response.

Only the moonlight listens wide-eyed.
Only the stars listen closely.

술맛 살맛

부글부글 넘친다
술잔 돌리는 벅찬 기분

추억처럼
보슬비 내리는 밤
매콤한 민어 냄새

아,
그 구수한 너의 살맛

Wine Taste Warm Taste

Simmering, sizzling it boils over,

Our mood brimming as we pass around the wine cup.

Like a memory

A misty rainy night

The peppery croaker aroma

Ah,

Your tasty warmth.

한 줄의 시
— 방곤* 선생님의 영전에 바쳐

1

길모퉁이 파리바게트 커피숍
빈자리 하나
한 줄기 담배 연기처럼
떠오르는

2

선생님의 빙글 얼굴
제자 · 동료 · 오랜 친구들의
분분히 쌓여 있는
선향과 꽃송이 사이로
미소 짓고 있는

3

하얀 시
한 줄

---

* 방곤 : 불문학자.

이 시대를 위한 우화

옛날 옛날 동해바다 속에
거북이 한 마리 살고 있었네
용왕의 병을 고치려고
토끼 간을 찾아
육지에 나갔다네
어떻게나 잘 속였는지
사로잡힌 토끼들
거북이 등에 빈틈없이 꽉 찼는데
공교롭게 관세 그물에 걸렸다네
밀수로 구속 기소되었는데
요즘도 거북이들 큰 집에 엉금엉금 기고 있네

조심하시라!
큰 고기도 그물은 뛰어넘지 못하나니……

자줏빛 꿈

1

산들산들 라일락 바람을 타고
할머니 집의 향수를 풍긴다

2

안방으로 들어가 어른들 몰래
화장대 위 크고 작은 병들의
독특한 냄새를 살금살금 맡고

3

뒤쪽에 낡은 항아리의 시퍼런 향기
할머니의 마음 한구석에 살며시 떠다니는 것처럼
내 이마에 스며든다

4

그리움에 적신 말린 꽃들이 다시 피고
옛 얼굴 오랜 생각 서서히 떠오른다
내 어린 시절의 보랏빛 꿈 가끔 꾼다

Grandmother' s Dressing Table

I go into the women' s quarters, while the grown-ups aren' t watching
And I stealthily sniff the peculiar aromas
Of the various bottles on the dressing table.
The blackish blue fragrance of an old bottle in the back
Furtively floating out of a corner of Grandmother' s heart
Unawares soaks into my brow
Seeps deep into my breast.

Bathed in homesickness dried flowers bloom again.
Bygone faces, lingering thoughts come to mind little by little.
These days I dream the lilac dream of my youth.

가을 출근길엔 특히 주의하시오!

가을바람에 흔들흔들 은행나무 행렬 따라
굽이굽이 낙엽을 쓸어 모으는 할아범
그들의 담배꽁초들과 뒤죽박죽의 버림치를
쓸어 내고 있다 산뜻하게

빗자루 꽉 잡은 굵은 손가락 마디
비뚤어진 혹투성이의 나무줄기들
그들의 한없이 쌓인 한평생의 죄를
맑게 씻어 낸다

일방통행……
주차 금지……
견인 지역……
쓰레기 무단 투기 특별 감시……
아무리 소리 높여 외쳐도 누구도 듣지 않는다

In the Fall, Pay Attention on the Way to Work!

Along the line of ginkgo trees swaying in the fall breeze
Grandpa rakes together the fallen leaves
Sweeps cigarette butts and discarded junk

The thick knuckles firmly grasping the broomstick
The tilted gnarled tree trunks
Freshly cleanse
The lifelong piles of sins.

One Way Traffic……
No Parking……
Tow Away Zone……
Illegal Rubbish Disposal Under Surveillance……
No matter how much you shout, no one
pays attention.

굴참나무 쉼터

아득히 먼 하늘에 봄 숨소리 들려서
철새 떼 내려와 가지가지에 앉는다
땅의 곡조를 따라서 뿌리의 숨결 깊어지고
마을 어귀 지키는 굴참나무 오랜 그늘에서

한 사나이 나무에 기대어
한 숨 한 숨 역사의 호흡을 엿듣고 있다

Resting Place at the Oriental Oak

Hearing the spring breath of the far-away sky
A flock of migratory birds descends and perches on each branch.
In tune with the earth' s song the breathing of the roots deepens
In the ancient shade of the oriental oak guarding the village entrance.

A man resting against the tree
Overhears the breaths of history, one at a time.

겨울밤

1

묵은 김치와 마늘과 깻잎 곁들여
그 보글거리는 토장국 내음
안방 화롯가에 옹기종기
군고구마처럼 따스하던 겨울밤

2

오래오래 남아 있다
지글거리는 할머니 두부찌개
그 옛날 같은 손맛의 그리움이

Winter Evening

Stale kimchee garnished with garlic, green onions, sesame leaves
That aroma of simmering soybean paste stew
We huddled around the charcoal brazier in the inner room
A winter evening as warm as a roasted sweet potato.

It lingers for a long, long time
Grandmother' s bubbling bean curd stew
A yearning for that old time hand-made taste.

오늘도 서울의 맥박은 뛴다

1

불꽃이 타오른다 엉클어진다
알 전류가 흐르고 있는
서울 가로의 은행나무 가지들

2

금속성과 신록의 살결이
쟁쟁쟁 부딪치고 있어
수십 볼트 전기와 초록 숨결이
끈질기게 얼싸안고 있어

3

광맥이 뚫려
푸르른 물결치는 서울 가로수의 바다

Today the Pulse of Seoul Throbs

Sparks flare up, get entangled.
Electricity flows through the Ginkgo tree branches
On Seoul streets.

Metallic and fresh green textures resonate and clash.
Thousands of volts of emerald breath tenaciously embrace.

A mineral vein is opening
An undulating blue-green ocean
Seoul street trees

개미 이야기

이봐요! 함부로 밟지 마요!
8월초 길거리 지글지글
싸움판이 벌어지고 있어.
버려진 콩나물 대가리 차지하려고
서로 밀치락달치락하는군요.
여름 용품 파격 세일 장터처럼
사람들아 무심코 짓밟지 말아요.
우리가 언제 황금연휴여행 했나요?
별장형 주말주택을 가져 본 적 있나요?
아이쿠! 어림없는 소리
한여름 내내 허리띠를 졸라매고
땀만 뻘뻘.

The Ants' Tale

Hey! Don' t tread on us!
On the sizzling early August street
A fight takes place
For discarded bean sprouts.
We push and shove each other
Like a summer supplies bonanza bargain sale.

Folks, don' t trample on us.
Did we ever take a golden holiday trip?
Have we ever owned a weekend resort cottage?
Not a bit! Far from it.
All summer long we' ve tightened our belts
Just streaming sweat.

디아스포라, 차별과 경계를 넘어서

김 재 홍
(문학평론가 · 경희대 명예교수)

온갖 아픔 진전시키는
우리 동네 안창식 약사

감기 기침 배탈 신경통
어린 투정 오랜 고민
하루도 빠짐없이
사알살 달래는 약손

이 시대의 울화병
누그러뜨리는 1. 2. 3 약국

—「1. 2. 3 약국」 전문

1. 현태리 시인 누구인가?

현태리THERESA HYUN 씨, 이분은 재미있는 이력을 지닌 사람입니다. 이탈리아 출신의 미국인이고, 미국 대학에서 프랑스 문학을 공부했으며, 한국의 경희대학교에서 불문학 교수로 재직하다가 지금은 캐나다 토론토의 요크대학교에서 비교문화, 한국시를 강의하고 있는 교수이자 시인이기 때문입니다.

그런가 하면 1990년대 여러 해 경남 통영의 수국시인학교에도 참여하고 1999년 백담사 만해축전 기간에 열린 한국문학 100년 국제학술심포지엄에서도 주제 발표를 하는가 하면 만해시인학교의 열성 회원이기도 한 한국과 한국인, 한국문학 특히 시를 사랑하는 분이기도 합니다. 요즘 말로 이른바 동서를 넘나드는 디아스포라 세계인, 지구촌인이라고 불러볼 수 있겠습니다.

무엇보다도 이분은 2003년 고은 시인의 추천을 받아서 계간 『시와시학』에 정식으로 등단한 외국인 출신 현역 시인이라는 점에서 특기할 만하다고 하겠습니다. 지금도 이분은 캐나다에 거주하면서도 세계 여러 나라에서 열리는 한국학 · 비교문학 국제학술심포지엄에 열성껏 참여하기도 합니다. 또한 캐나다 토론토 현지에서 한국 인문학회에 성심성의로 참가하고 열심히 한글 시를 창작 · 발표하는 한편 해마다 설악산 만해축전과 시인학교에 참여하는 것을 기쁨이자 자랑으로 아는 그야말로 한국과 한국인 · 한국 문학을 사랑하는 고마운 분이기도 합니다.

이런 분이 이번에 한글로 시집을 출간한다고 해설을 청탁하기에 한국인의 한 사람으로서 우선 놀랍기도 하고 한편으로는 세계화Globalization 시대에 인류 가족, 세계인 가족의 일원으로서 고맙기도 합니다. 한국 · 한국인을 사랑하고 공부하는 분들이 적지 않은 21세기 오늘날에도 THERESA HYUN 교수, 아니 현태리 시인만큼 진정으로 한국을 사랑하고 한국인의 정서를 깊이 이해하고 애정을 갖고 연구하면서 등단까지 하여 한국어 시를 직접 창작하는 경우는 그 예가 아직까지 없는 것으로 알기 때문입니다.

특히 현대시란 그 나라 민족, 모국어 사용자native speaker들도 제대로 이해하기 어렵고, 더구나 직접 창작을 하기는 어려운 일이기에 놀랍고 신기한 것입니다. 시는 한 민족, 한 언어에 있어 최상의 발화 양식이기에 시를 창작하려면 가장 높은 정신 활동을 이해할 수 있어야 하며 그 감수성까지도 섬세하게 감응해 낼 수 있어야 하는 것이기 때문에 누구나 쉽게 접근할 수 없는 것이기 때문이지요.

그동안 어렵게 한국 시, 한국 역사, 사회문화를 직접 겪으면서 한국인의 사상 · 감정을 애정을 갖고 깊이 있게 공부하여 마침내 첫 창작시집 『판문점에서의 차 한잔』을 상재하는 현태리 시인을 축하하고 격려하는 뜻에서 간략하게나마 그 시세계를 살펴보기로 합니다.

2. 한국적 풍정과 한글의 표정성

먼저 이 시집은 우리에게 한국적인, 너무나 한국적인 풍정으로서 서울 거리를 만나게 해 주어 관심을 환기합니다.

겨울 내내
네거리에

찬바람 퇴근길에 고구마 좀 사려 하니
할머니 웃으면서 천 원어치 골라 주네

겨울 내내
네거리에

머얼리 눈 덮인 산 바라보면
옛사람 옛이야기 생각나네

겨울 내내
네거리에

거스름 돈 쥐어 주는 군고구마 같은 손
그냥 웃으며 하염없이 살아가네

—「고구마 할미」 전문

쉽게 다가오는 시지요? 평범한 서울 가로에서 고구마를 파는 할머니와 그 고구마를 사면서 느끼는 이방인의 애틋한 정감을 소박하게 노래한 시인 것입니다.

그런데 여기에서 먼저 공감하게 되는 것은 "찬바람 퇴근길에 고구마 좀 사려 하니/ 할머니 웃으면서 천 원어치 골라 주네"라는 인정 어린 삶의 풍정이며, "머얼리 눈 덮인 산 바라보면/ 옛사람 옛이야기 생각나네"에서 불 수 있는 과거적 상상력의 발현입니다. 그러면서도 "거스름돈 쥐어 주는 군고구마 같은 손/ 그냥 웃으며 하염없이 살아가네"라는 결구에서 보듯이 "군고구마 같은 손"과 같은 맛깔스런 관찰력과 표현력, 그리고 "그냥 웃으며 하염없이 살아가네"라는 한국적 체념과 달관을 읽어 내는 통찰력과 내면화하는 솜씨는 그냥 외국인의 단순한 이국정서를 넘어서서 한국인의 내밀한 정신세계를 들여다보고 있다는 점에서 관심을 끄는 것이 아닐 수 없습니다.

이른바 체념과 달관 또는 비관적 낙관주의라고 하는 한국인 특유의 정신적 내면 풍경을 드러내 보여 준다는 점에서 주목할 만하기 때문입니다. 특히 "군고구마 같은 손"이라는 구절에서 엿보이는 한국적 얼굴과 언어의 표정성은 한 수준을 이루고 있으며 현태리 시인의 한국적 정서와 한국어 감응 능력을 짐작케 해 주기에 충분한 것으로 판단됩니다.

3. 사주팔자를 2만 원에 사고판다고요?

그런데 이러한 시인의 한국적 정서와 한글 표현 능력은 보편적인 정도를 넘어서서 하나의 미학적 수준을 이루어 가고 있다는 점에서 주목할 만합니다.

① 점쟁이를 찾아볼까요?

그래그래
돈암 고갯길 아래
매연 속 얼핏 보이는
팔자 신수 궁합 간판의 숲
들여다볼까요?

언제나 문은 열려 있고
안방에 그윽이
사주책 잡은 손 더듬더듬
오십 평생 눈먼 세월
손으로 한번 볼까요?

앞길 어두컴컴하니
걸음걸이 밝히자
때로는 만 오천
때로는 이만 원어치 사주팔자를 산다

생生의 바다 등불을 찾아볼까요?

—「점쟁이를 찾아서」 전문

② 아득히 먼 하늘에 봄 숨소리 들려서
철새 떼 내려와 가지가지에 앉는다
땅의 곡조를 따라서 뿌리의 숨결 깊어지고
마을 어귀 지키는 굴참나무 오랜 그늘에서

한 사나이 나무에 기대어
한 숨 한 숨 역사의 호흡을 엿듣고 있다

—「굴참나무 쉼터」 전문

③ 부글부글 넘친다
술잔 돌리는 벅찬 기분

추억처럼
보슬비 내리는 밤
매콤한 민어 냄새

아,
그 구수한 너의 살맛

—「술맛 살맛」 전문

인용 시가 그렇지 아니합니까?

먼저 시 ①은 돈암동 미아리고개 어디쯤이 그 배경인 듯하지요. "사주책 잡은 손 더듬더듬/ 오십 평생 눈먼 세월/ 손으로 한번 볼까요?"라는 사주, 팔자, 관상, 손금을 통해서 인생의 화복길흉은 물론 전생과 현생, 내생을 비추어 보려는 한국인의 심서를 꿰뚫고 있는 것입니다. 특히 "때로는 이만 원어치 사주팔자를 산다"라는 구절에서 볼 수 있는 한국어 감각과 표현 능력, 그리고 "생生의 바다 등불을 찾아볼까요?"라는 인식의 폭과 깊이는 돋보이는 풍경이 아닐 수 없습니다.

시 ②도 그렇지요. "아득히 먼 하늘에 봄 숨소리"라거나 "땅의 곡조를 따라서 뿌리의 숨결 깊어지고"라는 시적 인식도 그렇지만 "마을 어귀 지키는 굴참나무 오랜 그늘", "한 사나이 나무에 기대어/ 한 숨 한 숨 역사의 흐름을 엿듣고 있다"라는 시적 표현은 웬만한 한국 시인들의 수준을 상회하는 것이라고 할 수 있을 겁니다.

특히 시 ③에서 "부글부글 넘친다/ 술잔 돌리는 벅찬 기분"을 느낀다거나, "추억처럼/ 보슬비 내리는 밤/ 매콤한 민어 냄새"를 "아,/ 그 구수한 너의 살맛"으로 받아들이며 "술맛 살맛"으로 육화시키는 솜씨는 가히 일품이라고까지 할 수 있는 것이지요.

한마디로 말해 한국인의 감수성과 인식 방법 그리고 한글 표현 능력이 외국인으로서의 호기심 또는 취미 정도를 넘어선 프로 수준에 육박하고 있다고 평가할 수 있겠습니다.

4. 현실 · 사회 응시와 비판 정신

그런가 하면 시인은 한국의 풍정에 대한 긍정과 함께 사회 현실 및 한국인의 삶에 관한 날카로운 인식을 통해 비판 정신을 펼치고 있어서 또 다른 관심을 환기합니다.

서초, 방배, 사당 역마다
조간신문을 옆구리에 낀
출근 행렬

바늘도 들어갈 틈 없는 열차 속
꽉 찼네 활짝 펼친 신문
펼쳐 든 신문 지면 속
내쳐지고 또 채워져

신촌, 이대, 시청 역마다
버려져 꾸깃꾸깃 내려져

파묻히는 일 속

—「동행」 전문

이 시가 그렇지요. 한국인들의 아침 출근 모습을 사실적으로 묘사하는 가운데 그 고단한 삶의 현실과 방법에 대한 비판적 인식을 보여 주고 있어서 관심을 끄는 것입니다.

그렇습니다. 대도시적 삶의 풍경으로서 출퇴근 지하철은 가히 지옥철이라고 불릴 정도로 "바늘도 들어갈 틈 없는" 게 사실입니다. 또한 그 틈바구니 속에서 너도나도 신문을 펼쳐 놓고, 휴대폰 귀에 대고 큰 소리로 떠들어 대고, 다 읽은 신문은 아무렇게나 팽개치고 내려서는 어딘가로 사라져 가는 그런 모습 아닙니까.

바로 이 지점에서 시인은 이러한 서울의 복잡하고 무질서 한 한 풍경 속에서 반생명력, 반인간적 풍경들을 날카로이 잡아내고 그에 대한 비판을 펼치고 있는 것입니다.

험악한 삶의 길에
여러 가지 주의 사항

공사 중!
 과속 단속
  전용차선
   추월 금지
    속도를 줄이시오
     추락 주의!
      위험!

앞만 보고 달려도 앞 못 보는
자동인형들

한남대교
 반포대교
  성산대교
   행주대교
    김포공항으로
     세계를 향해

      서울이 추락한다

—「서울 테러리스트」 전문

이러한 대도시적 혼란상은 세계 어디서나 흔히 볼 수 있는 것이 사실입니다. 그런데도 현태리 시인에겐 유독 불안하고 위태로운 모습으로 다가오는가 봅니다. "공사 중!/ 과속 단속/ 전용차선/ 추월 금지/ 속도를 줄이시오/ 추락 주의!/ 위험!" 이러한 위협적인 경고문들이 범람하는 서울의 대도시적 징후는 실상 선진 외국인들에게 위험하게 느껴지고 불안 심리를 자극하는 요인들이었을 것입니다.

또한 "한남대교/ 반포대교/ 성산대교/ 행주대교/ 김포공항으로/ 세계를 향해"라는 구절들 속에는 지난날 '성수대교' 사건이 암시하는 부실공사와 각종 대형사건 · 사고에 대한 각성을 촉구하는 게 아닐 수 없을 것입니다. 그러기에 세계화의 구호 속에서 서울은 무너지기 쉬운 하나의 '사상누각' 으로서 인식되기도 하며 그 결과 "서울이 추락한다"라는 결구를 형성하면서 '서울 테러리스트' 라는 자극적인 제목을 붙이게 된 것이 아니겠습니까?

아울러 한국인들을 일에 몰려 "앞만 보고 달려도 앞 못 보는/ 자동인형들"로 인식함으로써 고도성장의 화려한 그늘에 가려져 삶의 참모습을 잃고 바삐바삐 살아가는 안타까운 모습에 대한 비판과 야유를 담고 있다는 점에서 그의 한국 사랑이 맹목적 · 피상적 · 감상적인 수준을 훨씬 넘어서고 있다는 사실에 유의할 필요가 있을 것입니다.

5. IMF와 판문점 사이에서

그런데 특히 그의 시에서 유의할 점은 시인이 한국 사회 현실뿐만 아니라 역사적 상황까지도 확실하고 또 깊이 있게 인식하고 있다는 사실입니다.

1
관광객 꽉 찬 휴게소
오랜만에 형제끼리 모였다
진달래 활짝 핀 봄날 오후

2
인파의 소용돌이 속
큰형님 창밖을 내다본다
……저 북쪽 흐린 하늘
보이지 않는 얼굴
……아직도 살아 있을까

3
두런두런 이야기들 하는데
큰형님 훌쩍 마시네
눈물 한잔

—「판문점에서의 차 한잔」 전문

'판문점' 이란 무엇이던가요? 한마디로 근대 한국사의 구조적 모순과 불합리의 대표적 상징이 아니겠는지요. 일제 강

점과 그로부터의 해방, 그리고 그에 이어진 좌우대립과 국토 양단 및 전쟁의 포연 속에서 생겨난 민족 비극의 상징이고 불행의 표상이라는 말씀입니다. 일본 제국주의의 패망과 전후 동서열강의 세계질서 재편 과정에서 폭발할 수밖에 없었던 한국전쟁과 민족분단 및 이산가족의 비극과 아픔, 슬픔의 표상에 해당한다는 말씀입니다.

그런데 여기에서 시인은 판문점을 흔히 많은 외국인들이 그러하듯이 일시적 호기심을 충족하거나 관광하는 차원으로서 바라보는 것이 아니라 그것을 통해 한국 · 한국인의 내면적 상처와 그 후유증을 심각하게 들여다보고 있어서 주목을 환기하는 것입니다. "저 북쪽 흐린 하늘/ 보이지 않는 얼굴/ ……아직도 살아 있을까?" 그리고 "큰형님 훌쩍 마시네/ 눈물 한잔"이라는 결구 속에는 한국인의 내면 깊이 자리한 역사적 상처와 현실적 아픔 및 슬픔이 예리하게 각인되어 있기 때문입니다.

비에 젖고 있는 기중기
우두커니 서 있다 꾸부정히
저 아래 길거리를 내려다보는
느티나무, 낮고 구슬픈 빗소리에
귀 기울이고 있다
비에 젖은 사내처럼

—「느티나무 비에 젖어—서울, 1998. IMF①」 전문

쏴쏴 장대비 쏟아져

고층 아파트에서 우듬지까지
천지만물이 울고 있는데
그 굵고 검은 몸통 앞에
담배만 애타게 태우는
한 젊은이
나뭇잎이 모진 눈물
한 방울 두 방울 받아들이고 있다

—「비–서울, 1998. IMF②」 전문

'판문점' 이 표상하는 역사적 상처와 그 후유증은 오늘날 한국이 처한 온갖 우여굴곡과 조응되면서 더 깊이 있고 날카롭게 한국의 비극적 현실을 응시하게 되어 설득력을 더해 줍니다.

1990년대 중반 맞이했던 외환 위기, 이른바 IMF 사태가 그것이지요. 국토 양단과 남북 민족 분단, 그리고 동 · 서 · 좌 · 우 분열과 대립상은 마침내 심각한 외환 위기와 경제 불안 및 사회 혼란을 야기하게 된 것이지요. 아니 이 IMF 사태는 단지 경제적 위기 상황을 넘어서서 20세기 한국의 정치 · 사회 · 문화가 당면한 총체적 위기와 불안의 상징이 아닐 수 없을 것이 자명합니다.

인용 시에서도 "비에 젖고 있는 기중기" 와 "비에 젖은 사내" 그리고 '비에 젖는 느티나무' 와 '장대비' '눈물' 등은 이러한 한국 사회의 총체적 난국과 위기 상황을 단적으로 암시한 것이라 하겠지요.

그렇게 보면 시 「판문점에서의 차 한잔」에서의 '눈물 한잔'

은 바로 역사적 모순과 부조리의 단적인 상징이며, 여기 시편들에서의 '비/장대비/모진 눈물' 은 한국 사회의 구조적 모순 및 불합리를 총체적으로 표상한 것이 아닐까 합니다. 일제 강점과 식민통치, 해방과 혼란, 전쟁과 분단 및 폐허 속에서 일궈 낸 경제적 성과가 근본적으로 흔들리는 상황을 맞이했던 까닭이지요.

이렇게 보면 현태리 시인의 한국 · 한국인 · 한국 사회 · 한국 역사에 대한 인식은 한국에서 네이티브 스피커Native Speaker들의 보편 수준을 넘어서는 정도이며, 그 시 또한 그런 수준으로 여겨진다는 점에서 의미가 있는 것으로 판단됩니다.

6. 맺음말—디아스포라, 경계와 차별을 넘어서

그렇다면 현태리 시인의 시는 한국문학인가, 아니면 영문학, 외국 문학에 속할 것인가요? 흔히 한국문학이라면 한국인이, 한국인의 사상 감정을, 한국어로 표현한 문학을 일컬어 온 것이 사실입니다. 그런데 이렇게 보면 현 시인의 시는 한국문학의 범주에 묶어 논의하는 것이 온당치 않은가 합니다. 필자는 현태리의 이번 시집을 엄연히 한국문학의 범주에 이끌어 들여야 한다고 생각합니다.

첫눈 오는 밤거리

발자국 따라가는데
문득 사라져 버리네
뒷골목조차 없는 이 도시
하얗게 덮여 있어

이 밤거리
내 언 손 감싸 주던
너의 입김
틈조차 없는 이 세상 밖으로
희미해져 가고 있네

눈길에 남아 있어
너의 새하얀 그림자

—「토론토 12월 거리에서」 전문

뿌리도 정처도 없는
한 떠돌이
땅속으로 깊이 내린
수백 년 달콤 씁쓸한 노래
마음으로 듣고 있다
빗속에 서성거리고 있다

—「장마—서울, 1998. IMF③」 전문

이 두 편의 시는 '한국인/외국인' '서울/토론토'의 경계와 차별을 넘어서 존재합니다. 말하자면 이 시집의 내용들은 국경과 인종과, 국적을 넘어서서 인간의 본원적인 운명의 형식으로서 그리움과 외로움, 그리고 그 속성으로서 허무 의식과 떠돌이 의식이 관류하고 있기에 인류 보편성에 근접하고 있음을 확인할 수 있습니다. 무엇보다도 영어가 모국어인 사람에게서 도저히 느낄 수 없는 한국적 내면의식과 한국적 정서를 깊이 있게 노래하고 있으며 한국어를 수준 높게 구사하고 있다는 점에서 한국문학이면서도 세계문학으로서 충분한 가능성을 보여 주는 것으로 판단됩니다.

말하자면 문학적 관습에 있어서의 제반 경계와 차별을 넘어서서 인류 보편성으로서의 문학, 세계문학 그 자체로서 형상화에 성공하고 있다는 뜻이 되겠습니다.

한국의 현역 시인으로서 현태리 시인, 그러면서도 세계적인 비교문학 학자로서의 현태리 교수의 능력이 잘 조화되어 앞으로 한국 시의 글로벌적인 시야 확대와 가치의 재발전이 이루어져 가길 기대하고 희망합니다.

Theresa Hyun Book of Poetry Review

BEYOND DIASPORA, DISCRIMINATION, BOUNDARIES

Kim Jay Hong

(Literary Critic, Professor Emeritus, Kyung Hee University)

Soothing all sorts of aches
Our neighbourhood pharmacist, An Ch' ang-Sik

Colds, coughs, indigestion, nervous tension
Childish grumbling, lingering distress
Everyday without exception
Gently stroking medicine hands
Calm the pent-up feelings of our time
1.2.3 Pharmacy

— "1.2.3 Pharmacy" full text

1. Who is poet Theresa Hyun?

Theresa Hyun is someone with an interesting life history. As an Italian American she studied French literature in the US and taught French literature at Kyung Hee University in Korea. Now she is a poet and professor of comparative culture and Korean poetry at York University in Toronto, Canada.

For several years she took part in the Kyongnam T' ongyong Suguk Poetry School, and in 1999 she presented a paper at the Paekdam Temple Manhae Festival during the 100th Anniversary of Modern Korean Literature Manhae Symposium. She is an enthusiastic member of the Manhae poetry school and she is fond of Korea, Korean people, and Korean literature, especially poetry. In today' s terms we can say she travels around the world, as an international person of the global village.

Above all it is worth mentioning that as a foreigner and an active poet she was recommended by poet Ko Un in 2003 and made her official literary debut in the quarterly *Si wa Sihak* (Poetry and Poetics). At the present time, while living in Canada she enthusiastically participates in international Korean Studies and Comparative Literature symposia held in various countries. We can be happy and proud that besides devotedly taking part in the local Toronto Korean Canadian Writers' Association and zealously writing Hangul poems, she also participates each year in the Sorak Mountain Manhae Festival and poetry school. We are certainly grateful for her love of Korea, Korean people and Korean literature.

As a Korean to receive this request to write a commentary for her poetry book is astonishing, besides I appreciate it as a member of the human family and the world family in the age of globalization. Even these days in the 21th century when there are many people who are fond of and who study Korea and Korean people, so far I know of no case like that of Professor Theresa Hyun, rather poet Theresa Hyun, who is so genuinely dedicated to Korea, so deeply understanding of and devoted to Korean emotions while doing research, making a literary debut and writing original Korean poems.

Modern poetry is particularly difficult even for a country' s own people and native speakers to properly understand. Moreover, creative writing is difficult, so this is remarkable and marvelous. Since Poetry is the highest verbal form of a people, and a language, it requires an understanding of the highest mental activity, and the ability to delicately respond to that sensibility. Therefore it is not something that everyone can easily approach.

While experiencing directly and with difficulty Korean poetry, Korean history, society, culture, she became devoted to and studied Korean people' s thought and emotions. Finally, in order to congratulate and encourage poet Theresa Hyun on the publication of her first book of poetry, *A Cup of Tea at P' anmunjom* I briefly examine her poetic world.

2. Korean Artistry and Hangul Expressiveness

First, in this poetry book we meet a Seoul street scene with such a Korean artistic sense that it arouses our interest.

> All winter long
> At the crossroads
> Coming home from work in the biting wind, I stop to buy some sweet potatoes.
> Smiling, Grandmother picks out 1000 won worth.
> All winter long
> At the crossroads
> As she gazes at the far-away snow-covered mountain
> People of bygone days, old stories come to mind.

All winter long
At the crossroads
Hand like roasted sweet potatoes give out change.
Still smiling she idles her time away.

— "Sweet Potato Grandma" full text

It' s an easily approachable poem, isn' t it? The poem simply sings of the melancholy felt by a stranger who buys a sweet potato from a sweet potato selling grandmother on an ordinary Seoul street.

However, this is what first arouses sympathy "Coming home from work in the biting wind, I stop to buy some sweet potatoes. / Smiling, Grandmother picks out 1000 won worth." We recognize an artistic sense of life. In "As she gazes at the far-away snow covered mountain / People of bygone days, old stories come to mind." an imagination of the past is revealed. And then in these concluding lines "Hands like roasted sweet potatoes give out change. / Still smiling she idles her time away." the phrase "Hands like roasted sweet potatoes" reveals an agreeable power of observation and expressiveness. The portrayal of Korean acceptance and farsightedness in "Still smiling she idles her time away" displays the insight and interiorizing skill which goes beyond a simple foreigner' s exotic mood. It is interesting to note the way in which the Korean private mental world is glimpsed.

The depiction of the acceptance and far-sightedness, and the pessimistic optimism of the characteristic Korean mental landscape is noteworthy. In particular the Korean countenance and linguistic expressiveness revealed in the phrase "Hands like roasted sweet potatoes" indicates that poet Theresa Hyun can be judged to have reached an ample level of responsiveness to Korean sentiments and language.

3. Buying and Selling 20,000 Won Fortune.

However, I would also like to point out that this poet' s Korean atmosphere and hangul expressive ability go beyond the general level to reach an aesthetic level.

Shall we visit a fortune-teller?

Yes, all right
At the bottom of Donam pass
Glimpsed through the smog
A forest of billboards - destiny, fortune, marital harmony
Shall we stop by?

The door is always open.
In the inner quarters, quietly
The hands holding the fortune-telling book touch and finger
A fifty-year lifetime passed in blindness
Shall we see by hand?

The path ahead is somber
So let' s brighten our step.
At times we buy 15,000
At times 20,000 won worth of fortune.

Shall we visit the lamplight of life' s ocean?

— "Visiting a Fortune-Teller" full text

Hearing the spring breath of the far-away sky
A flock of migratory birds descends and perches on each branch.
In tune with the earth' s song the breathing of the roots deepens
In the ancient shade of the oriental oak guarding the village entrance.
A man resting against the tree
Overhears the breaths of history, one at a time.

— "Resting Place at the Oriental Oak" full text

Simmering, sizzling it boils over,

Our mood brimming as we pass around the wine cup.
Like a memory
A misty rainy night
The peppery croaker aroma
Ah,
Your tasty warmth.

— "Wine Taste Warm Taste" full text

Aren' t the quoted poems like that?

First, the background of poem (1) seems to be Donam dong Miari Hill. "The hands holding the fortune-telling book touch and finger / A fifty-year lifetime passed in blindness / Shall we see by hand?" Through fortune, destiny, face reading, palm reading light is shed on life' s happiness or misery, good and bad luck, past life, present life and next life, and the deep thoughts of Korean people' s minds are penetrated. Especially in the line "At times 20,000 won worth of fortune" Korean language sensibility and expressive ability can be seen. And "Shall we visit the lamplight of life' s ocean?" is a scene which shows the breadth and depth of perception.

Poem (2) is also like this. While "Hearing the spring breath of the far-away sky" or "In tune with the earth' s song the breathing of the roots deepens" display poetic awareness, the lines "In the ancient shade of the oriental oak guarding the village entrance", "A man resting against the tree / Overhears the breaths of history, one at a time." exceed the level of poetic expression which is satisfactory for Korean poets.

Especially in poem (3) when we understand the skill of the lines "Simmering, sizzling it boils over, / Our mood brimming as we pass around the wine cup.", "Like a memory / A misty rainy night / The peppery croaker aroma" "Ah, / Your tasty warmth", "Wine Taste Warm Taste" might well be considered a gem.

In a word a Korean person's sensibility, the manner of perception and the hangul expressive ability go beyond the level of a foreigner's curiosity and pastime and can be evaluated as coming close to the pro level.

4. Realism, Society, Steady Gaze, Critical Spirit

Our interest is also aroused by the fact that the poet, while affirming Korean artistry, also exhibits a critical spirit through the sharp awareness of social reality and the life of Koreans.

> Socho, Pangpae, Sadang, station after station
> The queue on the way to work

Morning newspapers inserted under arms

The train is chockfull of spread out newspapers
Without an inch to breathe.
In the midst of the expanding pages
They are cast away and crammed in.

Sinch' on, Edae, Shich' ong, station after station
They' re thrown away, crumpled. They' re dropped off.
Buried in work.

— "Traveling Together" full text

This is such a poem. As it realistically describes the scene of Koreans on the way to work in the morning, it elicits interest since it shows a critical awareness of the real conditions and manner of weary life. That' s right. To the extent that the subway might well be called the hellway, as part of the big city life scene going to and returning from work, "Without an inch to breathe" is the truth. Also, in that narrow space you and I both spread out newspapers, hold our cell phones to our ears and loudly make noise.

Crumpled newspapers are thrown away anywhere and we disappear somewhere. Isn' t this the image?

At this point the poet, in the midst of such a crowded and chaotic Seoul scene, sharply points out and expresses criticism of the anti-life force and inhuman scenes.

On the rugged path of life
Various warnings

Under Construction!
Speed Control Zone
Restricted Vehicle Lane
Passing Prohibited
Reduced Speed
Beware of Falling
Danger!

Automatic Dolls
Dash forward without seeing.

Hannam Bridge
Panp' o Bridge
Songsan Bridge
Haengju Bridge
Towards Kimp' o Airport
Heading for the world

Seoul is crashing.

— "Seoul Terrorists" full text

Such chaos of a large city can readily be seen anywhere

is the world. Even so it seems that poet Theresa Hyun feels uniquely uneasy and imperiled.

"Under Construction! / Speed Control Zone / Restricted Vehicle Lane / Passing Prohibited / Reduced Speed / Beware of Falling / Danger!" Such menacing warnings which flood Seoul as a sign of a large city can in fact make a foreigner feel endangered and stimulate an uneasy mental state.

Also, the lines "Hannam Bridge / Panp'o Bridge / Songsan Bridge / Haengju Bridge / Towards Kimp'o Airport / Heading for the world" suggest the Songsu Bridge incident, and urge awareness of faulty construction and various large accidents. So there is a realization that under the slogan of globalization Seoul is a "castle in the air" which can easily collapse, and formulating the line "Seoul is crashing" leads to the provocative title "Seoul Terrorists." Isn't this the case?

In addition, Koreans are driven by work. The lines "Automatic dolls / Dash forward without seeing." criticize and ridicule the fact that concealed in the magnificent shadow of high growth the true form of life is being lost, and the way of life is hasty and distressing. It is notable that the poet's love of Korea goes far beyond a blind, superficial and emotional level.

5. Between IMF and P'anmunjom

However, a particularly noteworthy point of her poems is the awareness not only of the actual situation of Korean society, but the definite and deep awareness of historical circumstances.

> At a resting place packed with tourists
> The family gathered after a long time
> On a spring afternoon azaleas in full bloom
>
> Amid the swirling crowd
> Oldest brother gazes out the window.
> -- That cloudy northern sky
> Those missing faces
> -- Could they still be alive?
>
> As they whisper together
> Oldest brother slowly sips
> A tea cup full of tears.
>
> — "A Cup of Tea at P'anmunjom" full text

What was "P'anmunjom"? In a word isn't it the representative symbol of the structural contradictions and absurdity of modern Korean history? It is the symbol of the liberation from Japanese occupation and then the resulting left-right confrontation and split of the country and the tragedy of the people which arose amidst the battle smoke of the war. It is the emblem of misery. It is the image corresponding to the inevitability of the Korean War, the division of the people, the tragedy of separated families, pain and sadness which exploded out of the defeat of Japanese colonialism and the post war reorganization of the world order by the great powers. However for the poet it is not like many foreigners who satisfy a temporary curiosity at the level of tourists. The poem is noteworthy for poignantly revealing the interior wounds and after-effects on Korea and the Korean people. In the lines "—That cloudy northern sky / Those missing faces / --- Could they still be alive?" and "Oldest brother slowly sips / A tea cup full of tears." there is sharply carved the image of the Korean people' s deep historical inner wound and actual pain and sadness.

A rain-drenched crane
Stands idly, slightly bent.
That Zelkova tree overlooking the street below
Listens carefully to the soft, sorrowful sound of the rain,
Like a rain-drenched man.

— "A Rain-Drenched Zelkova Tree" full text

The swishing rain pours down.
From high-rise apartments to tree tops
Heaven, earth and all creation weep.
In front of that thick, dark trunk
A young man anxiously smoking cigarettes
Receives the merciless tears one by one.

— "Rain" full text

"P' anmunjon" , representing the historical wound and after-effects, contributes to the persuasiveness of the steady gaze at the current Korean situation facing various complications corresponding deeply and keenly to Korean tragic reality.

The foreign exchange crisis of the mid 1990s is the IMF situation. The split of the country and the North-South division of the people, and the East-West, left-right division and confrontation finally brought about the severe foreign exchange crisis and the economic uncertainty and social chaos. It is self-evident that the IMF situation went beyond a simple economic crisis and symbolizes all the urgent 20th century crises and uncertainties in Korean politics, society and culture. In the quoted poems as well "A rain-drenched crane" , "a rain-drenched man" , "the rain-drenched Zelkova tree" , "The swishing rain pours down" , "tears" and so forth frankly suggest the general difficulties and crisis situations of Korean society.

Considered in this way, in the poem "A Cup of Tea at P' anmunjom" "A tea cup full of tears" is a direct symbol of historical contradictions and absurdities, and in "Rain" "Rain/ the swishing rain / merciless tears" generally represent the structural contradictions and absurdities of Korean society. Japanese occupation and colonial rule, liberation and chaos, war and division and the economic outcome amidst ruin are the reasons for encountering the basically unstable situation.

If we look at it this way, poet Theresa Hyun' s historical awareness of Korea, Korean people, and Korean society goes beyond a Korean native speaker' s general level. We can conclude that it is meaningful to consider these poems at this level.

6. Concluding Remarks : Beyond Diaspora, Boundaries, Discrimination

Then, do the poems of Theresa Hyun belong to Korean literature or English literature or foreign literature? It is true that usually when we say Korean literature we are referring to Koreans, Korean thought and emotions, literature expressed in Korean. But, if we look at it this way it is not appropriate to discuss poet Hyun' s poetry in the category of Korean literature. This writer thinks that this book of poetry by Theresa Hyun clearly must be included in the category of Korean literature.

On a night street as the first snow falls
I follow the footprints.
Unexpectedly they fade away.
This city without even a back alley
Is covered in white.

On this night street
Enveloping my frozen hands
Your breath
Becomes misty
In this world without even a gap.

Your pure white shadow
Remains on the snow-covered street.
— "On a Toronto Street in December" full text

Without roots or destination
A wanderer
Listens wholeheartedly to the bitter-sweet ancient song
Rooted deep in the earth.

Restlessly she paces back and forth in the rain.

— "Rainy Season, Seoul 1998" full text

These two poems exist beyond the boundaries and discrimination of Korean / foreign, Seoul / Toronto. To put it plainly, the content of this book of poems goes beyond borders, ethnic groups, nationality. Since these poems are suffused with the basic human destiny of yearning and solitariness and the attributes of emptiness and wandering, they approach what is universally human.

More than anything, these poems sing of Korean inner awareness and emotions which can hardly be experienced by a native English speaker. When we consider that they freely use Korean, we can conclude that they have the full potential to belong to Korean literature and world literature. To put it plainly, they go beyond various boundaries and forms of discrimination in literary usage and succeed in taking the form of universal human literature and world literature.

I anticipate and hope that, in the future, as an active poet of Korea as well as an international scholar of comparative literature Theresa Hyun' s abilities will harmonize to achieve an expansion of the global vision and a redevelopment of the value of Korean poetry.

시인 현태리

미국 아이오와 주립대학교에서 불문학 박사
프랑스 파티에대학교 초빙교수 역임
경희대학교 외국어대 전임교수 역임
2003년 『시와시학』으로 한국문단에 시인으로 등단
캐나다 요크대학교 한국학과 창설
현재 토론토 요크대학교 인문학부 교수
캐나다 한인문인협회 회원

주요 저서 :
『번역과 한국근대문학』, 시와시학, 1992.
『번역과 현대화 과정』, 동경 : 동경대출판부, 1995.
『한국여성작가론—식민지 시대의 번역과 여성주의』, 호놀룰루 : 하와이대학 출판부, 2004.
『번역과 창작—한국근대여성작가를 중심으로』, 김해동 역, 이대출판부, 2004.

Theresa Hyun

Biographical Sketch

Ph.D. French Medieval Studies, University of Iowa
Lectrice, Faculte des Lettres et des Langues, Poitiers
Professor, College of Foreign Languages, Kyung Hee University, Seoul
Current Position, Professor, Department of Humanities, York University, Toronto

Representative Publications :
1992 *Translation and Early Modern Korean Literature,* Si wa Sihaksa, Seoul
1995 *Translation and Modernization,* University of Tokyo Press, Tokyo
2004 *Writing Women in Korea : Translation and Feminism in the Colonial Period,* University of Hawaii Press, Honolulu

2003 *Si wa Sihak* New Poet Award
Member, Korean Canadian Writers' Association

판문점에서의 차 한잔

A Cup of Tea at P'anmunjom

지은이 | 현태리
펴낸이 | 김재돈
펴낸곳 | 도서출판 시와시학
1판1쇄 | 2012년 4월 30일
출판등록 | 2010년 8월 10일
등록번호 | 제2010-000036호
주소 | 서울 종로구 명륜동1가 42
전화 | 744-0110
FAX | 3672-2674

값 8,000원

ISBN 978-89-94889-31-3 03810